The Baseball Book

D0132048

The Baseball Book

A Young Player's Guide to Baseball

Kevin Briand

FIREFLY BOOKS

A FIREFLY BOOK

Published by Firefly Books (U.S.) Inc. 2003

Copyright © 2003, 2002 by Kevin Briand

All rights reserved. No part of this publication may be reproduced, stored in a retrieval system or transmitted in any form or by any means, electronic, mechanical, photocopying, recording or otherwise, without the prior written permission of the publisher.

First Printing

CATALOGING-IN-PUBLICATION DATA (U.S.)

Briand, Kevin.
   The baseball book : a young player's guide to baseball / Kevin Briand. — 1st ed.
[120] p. : col. photos. ; cm.
Includes bibliographical references and index.
Summary: The fundamentals of baseball with easy-to-understand instructions and step-by-step photography.
ISBN 1-55297-708-0
ISBN 1-55297-690-4
1. Baseball. I. Title.
796.357 21   CIP GV867.4.B75 2003

Published in the United States in 2003 by
Firefly Books (U.S.) Inc.
P.O. Box 1338, Ellicott Station
Buffalo, New York, USA
14205

Published in Canada in 2002 by Key Porter Books Limited.

Design: Peter Maher
Electronic formatting: Jean Lightfoot Peters
Illustrations: John Lightfoot
Additional material for Chapter 1: Michael Baginski

Printed and bound in Canada

To my mom and dad, for introducing me to baseball at a young age, encouraging me to play, and never putting any pressure on me to succeed; to all of my former coaches, especially John Haar, who gave me an environment conducive to learning and an opportunity to play the game that I love; and to my wife, Birute, and son, Richard, for being the best family one could ever have.

Contents

Foreword

As a young boy growing up in California, baseball was a large part of my life. My friends and I took advantage of every single chance we got to play. Baseball was a way of life for me back then, and it still is today. No game combines the thrill of one-on-one competition and the camaraderie of being part of a team quite like baseball. The pace, sounds, character and competition make it what it is—the greatest game in the world.

I played in little league, in highschool, at the junior college level, in the minor leagues, and ultimately, in the major leagues. I was a catcher, and although I possessed a tremendous amount of ability I never would have been able to get to where I did without some quality instruction and coaching. My major league career lasted for seventeen seasons and I was lucky enough to be coached by some of the best people in the business, including Whitey Herzog and Bobby Cox. My coaches helped me learn new drills and techniques. They also played an important role in passing along some key life skills. I think that I became a much more mature and confident person due to my early experiences with baseball.

When I was growing up, we didn't have many books and videos to help us learn the fundamentals of the game—although they would have made it easier to determine if we were doing something correctly or incorrectly. *The Baseball Book* will help you do just this. If you want to begin playing baseball, this book will give you a unique opportunity to learn. With informative, easy-to-understand instructions and step-by-step photography, *The Baseball Book* will take you through the fundamentals of the game—hitting, baserunning, throwing and receiving, and pitching. It will also offer information on areas that are often neglected: warm up and stretching, signing up, and the fascinating history of the game.

It is my hope that *The Baseball Book* will encourage you and your friends to play baseball and to learn as much as you can about this exciting game. Wherever your baseball experiences take you—whether its to the neighborhood ballpark or the major leagues—I hope you have as much fun as I've had.

Buck Martinez
Manager,
Toronto Blue Jays

In baseball, as in any other sport, improving your skills takes time and patience. Results will come with plenty of practice and repetition. Mark McGwire, Sammy Sosa and Barry Bonds weren't homerun kings when they started—they practiced long and hard to learn how to hit the ball out of the park. And Roger Clemens probably threw quite a few balls and wild pitches before learning how to hit the strike zone consistently. It takes time to perfect these skills, whether you're playing in the major leagues or in your own backyard.

The first time I played baseball was a total fluke. I was watching my older brother's team take on a team that was one player short. They asked me to play, and after some resistance, I gave in. I was put in left field that day, and didn't even have to catch a ball. I did, however, get one at-bat. I hit a double to

Sammy Sosa of the Chicago Clubs hits a home run during the All-Star Game Home Run Derby in Seattle on July 9, 2001.

Kevin Briand during his days at the National Baseball Institute in British Columbia, Canada. This shot was taken in 1991.

left-center field. The feeling of making solid contact with the ball was one of the best I've ever had.

I was ten years old when I started playing on a team, and I found that my skills lagged behind these of most of the other kids my age. Sure, I knew how to catch, throw, hit and run, but I'd learned most of that from watching games on television. I soon found out that even though I had plenty of raw ability for my age, there was a lot that I didn't know—and it took me a long time to catch up.

As I grew up and continued to play, I discovered I loved chasing down fly balls and throwing runners out at third or home. One day, when I was thirteen, my coach stopped me on the way to the ballpark. He told me that I would be the starting pitcher. I was terrified. Sure, I had a strong arm, but could I throw strikes? But I soon found out that I was meant to pitch. My ability on the mound led me to provincial all-star teams, Junior Team Canada and Team Canada. I played in the World Championships and received a

scholarship to the National Baseball Institute in Vancouver, British Columbia. I was able to travel the world, meet terrific players and have a wonderful time doing what I loved to do.

In those days, however, there wasn't a lot of information on drills and good technique. Had I known about proper delivery, or about what pitches I should or should not have been using, I might have been able to avoid the injury that led to the end of my pitching career. Luckily, it didn't end my baseball career. I still coach and work with amateur baseball organizations, and I'm a talent scout for the Toronto Blue Jays.

As a scout, I often see kids who have plenty of ability. It's too bad that many of them also have significant mechanical or technical problems that prevent their progress. What I really like to see are prospects with solid technique and potential. If good technique and mechanics are taught at a young age—when they are much easier to learn—the player will benefit, and his or

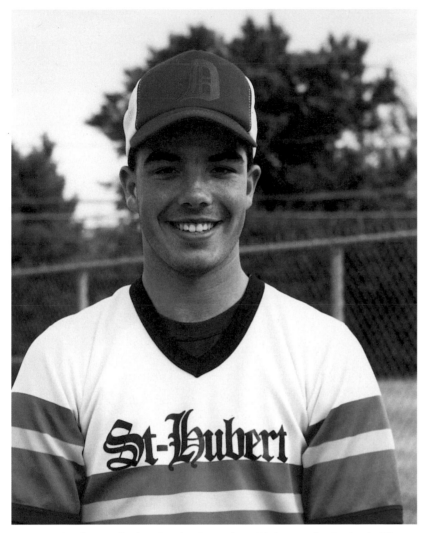

At 17, Briand was playing for the St. Hubert Diplomats in Quebec's Elite Baseball League.

and accompanied by photographs so that you can both read and see how a particular skill should be performed. Applied properly, this information will help you make the transition from an enthusiastic young baseball beginner to a knowledgeable young baseball player.

One note before we begin: Even though I recommend that each skill be taught and practiced in a certain way, this does not mean that there aren't different ways of doing the same thing. Your coach may recommend something different—and that's okay.

I hope that once you've learned how to perform some of these drills and have worked hard at perfecting your skills, you will find even more enjoyment in playing what I believe to be the greatest game in the world. And, once you get started, who knows where you'll end up?

her chances of improving will increase.

This book is meant to offer a simple and easy approach, so that someone who has never picked up a baseball will know how to begin. You'll find demonstrations of what many coaches believe to be the proper technique in several skill areas. Each subject will be broken down into simple steps

Nothing is quite like baseball. If you've ever played, you already know that there's no better feeling than hitting a ball on the sweet spot of the bat and watching it travel over the fence for a homerun, or striking out the last batter to win a game. More than any other sport, baseball is made up of magical moments—each one special to both the team and the individual player.

Baseball is one of the most-loved sports in the world. It's played in Latin America and Canada, in Japan and the United States. In North America, it's so popular that from April through October a major league baseball game can be see on television almost every day or night. When they are not watching games, or listening to them on the radio, hundreds of thousands of kids like you are playing on teams of their own—either through organ-ized leagues, or on baseball diamonds in neighborhood parks and schoolyards. So what's the big deal? What is it about baseball that makes people love it so much?

The History of Baseball

On the surface, baseball is a simple game: throw, hit, catch and run. It's not hard to imagine then that the game may have existed in one form or another since the days of the cavemen.

While there is no documented evidence of prehistoric men clubbing coconuts with a dinosaur bones, there is written evidence dating back as far as 1085 in England of games similar to baseball—although it's doubtful that William the Conqueror knew how to turn the pivot on a double play!

Since then, there have been games based around running, throwing, hitting and catching a ball. Two of the most popular were the British games of cricket and rounders, both of which are believed to have influenced the modern game of baseball.

The "National Pastime"

That game began to take shape in the United States in the early 1800s, when references to "base-ball" were already appearing in print. By the mid-nineteenth century, the game was already considered America's "national pastime."

The first official baseball team—the New York Knickerbockers—was formed by Alexander Joy Cartwright in 1842 (it's curious that, today, the "Knicks" are a basketball team), and it was Cartwright and his teammates who began to formalize the rules of the game as we know them today. (The widely held belief that Abner Doubleday founded the game is simply untrue.)

An Organized Sport

As the years passed, other teams formed to compete

Alexander Joy Cartwright.

against the Knickerbockers, and in 1857 the first amateur league—The National Association of Base Ball Players—was formed. Even

The New York Knickerbockers, 1845.

The 1933 American League All-Stars.

teams in Toronto and Hamilton, Ontario, had begun to play. In 1869, the Cincinnati Red Stockings became the first professional team, and in 1876 the National League went professional, too. A rival American Association was launched in 1882, but it wasn't until 1903 that the first World Series was played.

Since then the rules of the game have changed little, although some key changes included the introduction of a livelier ball, the first All-Star game (1933), night games (1935), and in 1947, the breaking of the color barrier, which allowed black players to play in the major leagues.

Today, television plays a major role in the game, players earn millions of dollars a year, and teams come and go. But, at its core, baseball is still a simple game, where players throw, hit, catch and run.

The Playing Field

Ballparks can be magical places, full of history and the memories of great baseball moments. Many boast their own unique dimensions and idiosyncrasies, making parks such as Boston's Fenway, with its "Green Monster" outfield fence, both historical and legendary. Yankee Stadium has a vegetable garden beyond the outfield fence, Kansas City's ballpark has its own waterfall and Toronto's SkyDome has a retractable roof. Still, each field is made up of the same basic elements.

The infield: While a baseball field is commonly referred to as a "diamond," that term rightfully applies only to the infield area. The proportions of all infields are constant, consisting of set dimensions that regulate the distance between the four bases—first, second, third and home—and the pitcher's mound in the center.

The bases: The infield is a square that is tilted into a diamond shape with home plate as the starting point,

first base to the right, second base opposite home and third base to the left. The distance between each base is 90 feet (27.4 m).

The pitcher's mound: In the center of the infield is a raised circular mound (18 feet/5.5 meters in circumference) from which the pitcher delivers his or her pitches to the plate. The pitching rubber marks the center of the mound, which is precisely 60 feet, 6 inches (18 m) from home plate.

The batter's box: The batter's box is shown by two chalk squares drawn on either side of home plate. This is where

the batter must stand while taking a turn at bat.

The foul lines: These chalk lines extend from home plate to first and third bases and beyond to the outfield fence, where they are then extended upwards as metal "foul poles." A batted ball must stay inside the foul lines/pole to be considered fair. A ball outside those lines is called a "foul ball" and is out of play. If a ball hits the foul pole, however, it's fair.

The baseline: This is the dirt track between bases that marks the path that the batter runs after a hit.

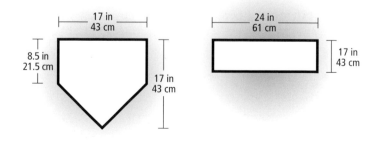

The dimensions of home plate and the pitching rubber.

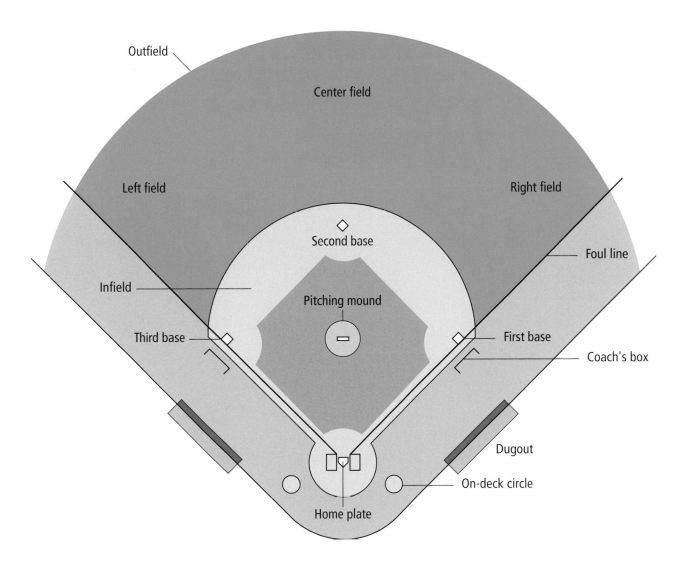

Outfield

Center field

Left field

Right field

Second base

Foul line

Infield

Pitching mound

Third base

First base

Coach's box

Dugout

On-deck circle

Home plate

The on-deck circle: The on-deck circle is a waiting area on the side of the infield. It's where the next batter up waits for his or her turn at bat.

The dugout: Players who are not required on the field sit on benches in the dugout—an area slightly below field level

under the stands. It also serves as the manager and coaches' "office" on the field.

The outfield: The term "outfield" refers to the vast expanse of field beyond the diamond that ends at the out-field fence.

The bullpen: The bullpen is the place where pitchers warm up before entering the game. It's usually situated beyond the outfield fence or along the outfield sidelines.

Getting Ready

Watching a major league baseball game can be a bit like listening to a different language. You'll hear commentators talking about at-bats, innings, the strike zone and the infield-fly rule. Don't be too confused. Behind all the fancy terms and strange rules, a game is waiting to be played—and won.

In baseball, a game is won when a team scores more runs than its opponents. A run is scored when a player suc-

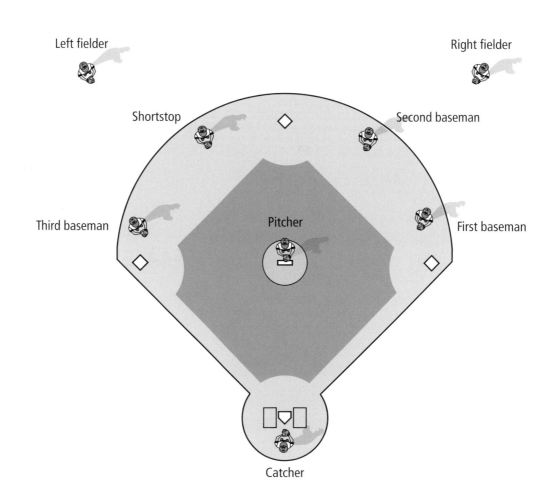

Center fielder

Left fielder

Right fielder

Shortstop

Second baseman

Third baseman

Pitcher

First baseman

Catcher

Player positions.

cessfully touches home plate after rounding the base path—touching all bases along the way—without being put "out."

Over the next four pages, you'll find some key information on how the game of baseball is played—and how those all-important runs are scored. Although the rules can change a little depending on where and at what level you play, the basics are pretty much the same.

Innings: Tops and Bottoms

At the major league level, a baseball game consists of nine innings, with teams taking turns in the field and at bat. Innings are divided into halves: during the "top" half of the inning, the home team takes its turn in the field, while the visiting team bats. During the "bottom" of the inning, the teams switch positions. If the game is tied after nine innings, additional innings are played until there is a winner. Unlike some other sports, a baseball game never ends in a tie.

There are only a few situations in which a major league game doesn't last nine innings. If the weather is horrible—like heavy rain or even snow, depending on when and where the game is being played—the umpire can "call" the game. And if the home team is winning in the top of the ninth, it doesn't need to play the bottom half of the inning. It may sound strange, but it makes sense. Remember, the home team bats in the bottom (second half) of the inning. If it's already winning in the top, it can't lose.

Player Positions

A player is described by the defensive station he plays. For example, the player at first base is called the first baseman. There are nine defensive positions: a pitcher on the mound; a catcher crouched behind home plate; infielders on first, second and third bases; a shortstop positioned between second and third bases; and three outfielders in right, center and left fields. If a player needs to leave the game, a new player may be substituted (the original player may not return). A substitute for the pitcher is called a relief pitcher.

When the team takes its turn at bat, players come to the plate according to a batting order that cannot be changed during the game—unless a player leaves due to injury or is pulled from the game by the manager. In this case, a substitute batter, known as a "pinch hitter" is assigned to the order. In the professional American League, a "designated hitter" takes the pitcher's place (pitchers are usually the weakest batters).

The Officials

Four game officials, or umpires, are stationed by each base to enforce the rules of the game. The home plate umpire has the final say on all calls. The game begins when the head umpire calls "Play ball!"

Play Ball!

All baseball games begin when the pitcher delivers a pitch across the plate to the catcher. The pitcher's goal is to throw the ball so that it passes through the "strike zone"—an area over the plate roughly between the hitter's knees and chest (the umpire has the final call). If he's successful, the pitch is called a "strike." If the ball crosses the plate outside of the strike zone, it's called a "ball."

Any pitch swung at but not hit is a strike, as is a ball hit foul. If a player has three strikes called against him during his at bat, he's "out" (unless his third strike comes on a foul ball; then, he gets to "stay alive" for at least one more pitch). Four balls constitute a "walk," which enables the batter to advance to first base. A player can also advance if hit by a pitch.

The strike zone.

Hitting the Ball

A batter can swing at any pitch, but he's only awarded a hit if the ball lands in fair territory without first being caught by a defensive player. If the batter reaches first base before the ball is fielded, it is called a single; reaching second base gives him a double, third base a triple, and a complete turn around the bases a homerun. A home run can also be scored if the ball is hit over the outfield fence within the designated foul lines.

Running the Bases

A batter who reaches base safely after a hit is called a "baserunner." Now, it's his job to advance all the way to home plate and score a run. He can do this when another player gets a hit or by "stealing" a base (running to the next bag when the pitcher delivers a pitch). Runners on first base must try to advance when a batter hits a ground ball. Runners on second or third must advance if the runner on the base before them is being forced to run.

You're Out!

An "out" can be registered in a number of ways: when a batter strikes out; when the ball is caught in the air by a defensive player; when the ball is caught by the first baseman (whose foot is on the bag) before the batter touches the bag; or when a runner who is off the base is "tagged" with the ball by a defensive player. A team's turn at bat is over when three outs are registered.

The Magic of Baseball

Now you've got the basics. You know a little about baseball's history, you know where it's played, and you know more than you used to know about how it's played. But as impor-tant as it is to know all of these things, they won't help you when it comes to discov-ering what makes baseball such a magical sport—a sport that many feel is the greatest game ever played. To under-stand that, you need to look a little deeper.

Strategy, Strategy, Strategy
Perhaps more than any other

Changing pitchers is just one way to strategize during a game. In the 1965 World Series, Minnisota Twins' manager Sam Mele signals to the bullpen for a new pitcher after the Dodgers banged Jim Kaat for two runs.

One of the longest games in baseball history began on April 18, 1981, continued into the wee hours of April 19 before being suspended. Play was finally finished—all 33 innings of it—on June 23. The teams, Rochester and Pawtucket, were from the International League, and this poor man had to score the whole thing!

sport, baseball is a game of strategy. Every time the pitcher steps to the rubber, he has a plan. Each pitch is thrown to a certain location with a certain speed and a certain movement. The defense plays a certain way depending on the count (the number of balls and strikes against the batter), the pitch being thrown, the batter at the plate, the score, the number of outs, and the number of runners on base. The hitter also has options. Should he bunt, hit and run, try for a walk, or wait for the pitcher to throw strikes? Even baserunners have the option of waiting for a safe hit or trying for the steal. Sound confusing? It may be at first, but once you learn the game, every at-bat becomes something thrilling, every pitch a chance to outsmart your opponent. For spectators, all of this drama makes for some pretty intense moments. Those that say baseball is a slow sport are only watching the clock!

One for All and All for One

Although baseball is played as a team—and can only be played well when the team works together—baseball players are in constant competition with themselves. Pitchers try to control the speed, movement and location of their pitches, not to mention getting batters out. Hitters, on the other hand, try to do one of the most difficult things in sport: hit a small, round ball with a long, thin bat. Their goal is to hit as often as possible, constantly raising their average—a figure that's calculated by dividing the number of hits by the number of at bats. The difficulty of this task has led some to call baseball a game of failure. Just think about it: the very best players in the major leagues hit for an average of .300 or slightly higher. This means that they are only hitting safely three out of every ten times they come to the plate. Imagine having that ratio in any other sport. You'd never make the team!

'Til the Fat Lady Sings

Have you ever heard the expression "It ain't over 'til the fat lady sings"? Although it actually applies to opera (another story entirely!), it's often said about baseball, too. Confused? Don't be. It's really pretty simple. The expression basically means that a game "isn't over until it's over" (a famous quote from Yogi Berra, a Hall of Fame catcher from the New York Yankees). Unlike hockey, basketball or football, baseball isn't played by the clock. There are no 20-minute periods or 15-minute quarters. A major league baseball game can last for a quick two hours, or a gruelling four. Barring bad weather or a natural disaster, a baseball game is only over when the last out has been recorded—not when the clock ticks off the last second.

Take Me Out to the Ballgame

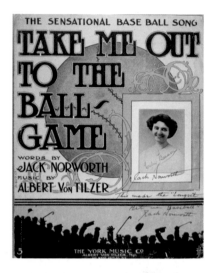

There's much more to baseball than balls and strikes. In fact, there are hundreds of references to the Grand Old Game in North American culture, including:

Songs

No trip to the ballpark would be complete without a rendition of "Take Me Out to The Ball Game."

> Take me out to the ball
>   game
> Take me out with the crowd
> Buy me some peanuts and
>   Crackerjack
> I don't care if I ever get back
>
> Let me root, root, root for
>   the home team
> If they don't win it's a
>   shame
> For it's one, two, three
>   strikes you're out
> At the old ball game!

Some teams—like the New York Yankees—use this popular tune to get fans on their feet during the 7th Inning Stretch. Others have written their own songs.

Comedy

The classic all-time baseball skit is Bud Abbott and Lou Costello's "Who's On First?" Straight-man Abbott is the manager who tries to explain that the names of his players include Who (on first base), What (on second), and I Don't

Yogi Berra.

Abbott and Costello performing "Who's on First?"

Know (on third). When poor Costello famously asks, "Who's on first?' Abbott replies: "Yes!" Things get pretty confusing after that.

Movies

There are dozens of movies about baseball, but in recent years Kevin Costner alone has made *Bull Durham, Field of Dreams* and *For the Love of the Game.* Some consider *Bang the Drum Slowly,* with Robert DeNiro, the finest baseball flick ever made. Others worth a look include *8 Men Out, Major League* and *The Bad News Bears.*

Books

More than 5,000 baseball books have been written, including classics like *Shoeless Joe* (which became the movie *Field of Dreams*) and *The Iowa Baseball Confederacy*, both by W. P. Kinsella. Other favorites with young readers include *Casey At The Bat: A Ballad of the Republic Sung in the Year 1888* (Handprint Books); *Cal Ripken Jr: Play Ball*, by Cal Ripken, Jr. and Mike Bryan (Puffin*); It's Baseball Season Again*, by Charles M. Schulz (HarperResource); and, *The New Dickson Baseball Dictionary*, by Paul Dickson (Harcourt Brace).

Over the years, ballplayers have been famous for their salty prose and colorful use of the English language—few more than the legendary Yogi Berra, who uttered the following head-scratching pronouncements:

"The game isn't over until it's over."

"Baseball is ninety percent mental. The other half is physical."

"You can observe a lot just by watching."

And lastly: "I never said most of the things I said."

Did you love playing catch when you were little? Was your favorite toy an inflatable ball? If you can't remember, ask your mom or dad what you were like as a small child. If you enjoyed throwing things—especially round objects—you may have been showing an early interest in baseball. The basic elements of the game—throwing, catching and running—come naturally to most kids. If you really *like* doing these things, though, the chances are good that you'll like baseball.

Even though you can learn many of the technical aspects of the game on your own, there's nothing like learning in an environment that will not only challenge you to compete but will also reward you for your accomplishments. Being on a team will help you make new friends, motivate you to improve your skills, and offer you the opportunity to learn from your teammates and your coach.

The First Steps

If you've decided to go ahead and give baseball a try, you'll need some proper equipment. Where would a National Hockey League forward be without his stick? Can you imagine a football player running down the field without his shoulder pads? Now picture this: You're catching for your team, and you're crouched behind the plate, ready to receive the pitch. How long do you think you'd last without shin guards, a chest pad, or a glove?

Although several positions come with unique equipment requirements—catchers have large gloves, so do first basemen—most ballplayers can start out with the basics.

Gloves, Balls and Bats

Since playing catch is how most baseball beginners begin (more about this in a minute), a glove is probably the best place to start. Your first glove doesn't have to be flashy or expensive—you're going to grow out of it in a few years—but it should be comfortable on your hand. Before you take it out to the diamond for the first time, remember to write your name and address on the inside tag. If you forget it somewhere after a game, it can be returned to you.

Next up is a ball. For beginners, a tennis ball or soft rubber ball is the way to go: if it hits you, it won't cause a cut or bruise. (Remember: if you're just starting out, you'll probably be missing a lot of catches!) As you get older and more experienced, try using a real baseball and see how you do.

You'll also need a bat. Getting the right bat is really important—the wrong kind can lead to injuries. Kids between three and seven should use foam bats. If you're eight or older, you can try out the aluminum ones. A batting helmet is another essential. Wear one whenever you're at the plate.

Playing Catch

So you've got your glove, your ball and your bat. What next? Playing catch is the first step in learning baseball skills. Once you are able to throw and catch a ball, the proper throwing and receiving actions

Playing catch is the first step in learning basic baseball skills.

can be taught. If you like baseball, you'll probably want to throw the ball all day long—to your friends or parents, up against a wall, or in the air. Always throw with the arm that feels most natural to you. When my son Richard was born, lots of my baseball friends asked me if I was going to teach him to throw left-handed (lefty pitchers are in short supply in the major leagues, making them pretty valuable players). I chose not to do this. Throwing should never been forced. When I was young, I started throwing left-handed because it felt more comfortable and less awkward. Figure out what feels right for

you and stick with it.

When throwing the ball, always play in a safe place to avoid accidents or injuries. If you're not sure if a place is safe, ask an adult. (For instructions on different ways to play catch, see Chapter 4.)

Batter Up!
Playing catch may be the best way to start learning baseball, but I bet you can't wait to hit, right? Hitting is the most popular part of baseball—who doesn't dream of knocking that game-winning home run over the center-field wall? The good news is that you can start hitting pretty early on— and the earlier you start, the

Hitting is the most popular part of baseball.

better you'll be over time. (To learn the basic elements of hitting, see Chapter 9.)

Signing Up

The decision to play organized baseball can be both exciting and confusing. You can't wait to get started, but finding information about local leagues, teams and organizations isn't always easy. How do you find out where to sign up and play?

Information about your local baseball association is often available at community centers, arenas, schools, swimming pools, post offices and other public places. When choosing your baseball program, remember that the best organizations and leagues emphasize having fun and learning how to play the game.

Another good way to gather information is to ask your friends. Do you know someone at school who plays baseball? Ask her how she got started. Is she playing with friends? Can you join in? If she's involved in T-ball, rookie ball or a recreation-center team, you can ask for more information or a phone number that you can call. If none of your friends are playing ball, try looking up different leagues on the internet or in the Yellow Pages. You can also look at the Baseball Contacts section on page 114 of this book.

Before you contact anyone, think about your goals for the baseball season. Do you want to have fun, learn, compete, win, all of the above, some of the above or none of the above? Figuring out what you want will help when it comes to making choices.

Making Choices

If you live in a large community, you may find that there are several baseball organizations or programs operating in your area. Don't be surprised if each has a different set of rules regarding age requirements, playing regulations, and boundaries (this can mean that if you live in a certain area you must play for a certain team). You'll also quickly find out that there's more than one type of baseball to play. Here are a few possibilities:

- T-ball offers an opportunity to hit the ball off of a batting tee without having to face a real pitcher. Players usually begin at age seven.
- Rookie Ball uses a pitching machine operated by a coach. Players are usually between the ages of seven and nine.
- Coach Pitch: Some leagues have the coaches pitch the ball to the hitters. Like Rookie Ball, the normal age range is between seven and nine.

Before You Register

With so many choices to make and so many things to consider, it's important to know what is being offered and whether it's right for you. Before registering, consider the following questions:

- **What is the total cost of the program?** Things like uniforms and equipment may not be included in the cost. You should know before you register what's covered and what isn't.
- **How many games and practices will there be?** This will tell you if your money is being well spent. Paying $100 for five games and no practices doesn't make a lot of sense.
- **On what days or nights will games take place?** Do you have piano lessons every Tuesday? If the team you're thinking of joining plays on Tuesday nights, you've got a problem. Talk to your parents and make sure that everyone in the family can work around the team schedule.
- **How many teams are in the league?** The more teams, the better. You don't get stuck playing the same team all the time, which can be a good thing if they're better than you!
- **How many players are on each team?** The ideal number of team members is between ten and twelve. Any less, and your team could end up forfeiting a game if someone is sick; any more and someone is going to be stuck on the bench.

Once you do decide to register, make sure that you have the phone numbers and e-mail addresses of your teammates and coaches. You'll need to reach them if you're going to miss a practice or a game, or if you need a lift to the park.

What to Expect

So, you've signed up for a team. Your first practice is still a week away, but it's all you can think about. You're excited, but you're a little nervous, too. Will you be the fastest on the team, or the slowest? Will you get along with your teammates? Will you win your first game, or be trounced by your opponents? All ball players worry about things like this, but you'll do fine if you concentrate on having fun and learning as much as you can. Look to your coach, the officials—including the umpire—and your teammates for help and motivation.

The Coach

There are many different types of coaches. Some are loud and talkative, some are soft-spoken and reserved. Some are great motivators, and some are teachers of the game. There are coaches that have all of these qualities, and coaches that have none. The head coach (or manager) is in charge of the team. She will make most of the decisions regarding the starting line-up, substitutions, strategy and discpline.

Listen to your coach's advice: you'll learn a lot about the game.

Your coach is an important part of your baseball experience. She'll decide how often you play, what defensive position you play, and where you hit in the line-up. A good coach will try to get all team members to play as much as possible—even though this isn't always easy. What makes a good coach? A good coach will:

- Encourage you to succeed
- Refrain from raising her voice or cursing
- Communicate well with you and your parents
- Communicate well with the other members of the team
- Have a good knowledge of baseball
- Be open to suggestions from players
- Be organized for games and practices
- Encourage a fun atmosphere
- Make coming to the park an enjoyable experience

As you get to know your coach, remember that she has a difficult job. Do what you can to make her work easier. Respect her judgment and listen to her advice; you'll learn a lot about the game.

The Umpire

Picture this: You're at the plate and the count is even at two balls and two strikes. The pitch comes across way off the plate—about a foot outside! You don't even bother to swing. But wait a minute! Is that the umpire yelling "strike three, you're out!"?

When you feel that the umpire has made a really bad call, it's hard to not to argue. But the next time you find yourself in a situation like this, stop and think about what a difficult and thankless job the ump has. Behind home plate, the ump has to call balls and strikes, and discipline players and coaches when they get out of line. She's involved in every single pitch of the game and often takes criticism from players, coaches and spectators. It's also up to her to call off the game in case of bad weather—not usually a popular decision. Out in the field, the game's other umpire decides whether runners are safe or out, and rules on fair or foul balls.

You may not always agree with the umpire working your game, but like a coach, she can help you out if treated with respect. Here are a few tips:

- Ask for the umpire's first name and use it. (Try to avoid using nicknames like "blue".)
- Never dispute an umpire's decisions on the field. Some umps can be vindictive when criticized. If you are unhappy with a call, talk to your coach and let her decide how to handle the situation. (If you don't react to a bad call, you just might earn the umps respect. Don't be surprised if the next difficult call goes your way.)
- Try to say "thanks" or "good game" as you leave the field.

Baseball Opportunities

In addition to being a great sport to play, baseball also provides some terrific job opportunities for young people across North America and around the world. Major league baseball players make an average salary of $2 million dollars per season! The best of the bunch—the Mark McGwires, Barry Bonds and Carlos Delgados—can also become celebrities. You'll see them endorsing products like juice, athletic equipment and credit cards; and you can bet they're well paid for their work!

You don't even have to make it to the majors to earn a living playing baseball. Although they don't make nearly as much as their major league counterparts, minor league players also earn a salary to play a game that they love—a game they've probably been playing for most of their lives.

Amateur and Recreational Baseball

In addition to being an Olympic sport, there are several important national and international competitions each year at different age levels. It is a great way to travel the world and make friends while doing something

Recreational ball is a great way to have fun and make friends.

that you love. If you'd like to know more about the various competitions, check with the organizations listed in the Baseball Resources section at the back of the book.

Recreational baseball is also a great way to spend a beautiful day outside, get some exercise, and meet new people.

The University of Baseball?

There may not actually be a University of Baseball, but the sport does provide an opportunity for young players to pay for all or part of their postsecondary school education. Many colleges and universities offer scholarships to players that they feel show potential. In addition to saving you (and your parents!) some money, these scholarships can make it possible for you to attend a school that might otherwise have been out of your reach.

A Different Way to Play

Not all baseball jobs involve picking up a bat and ball. All major and minor league clubs employ full-time coaches, scouts, front office personnel, trainers, doctors, clubhouse

Talented young players are sometimes offered scholarships to colleges or universities.

staff and ground crews. You may not make it to the big leagues as a player, but there are many other ways to be part of a team. If you read the Preface, you'll remember that I started out as a player and ended up as a manager of amateur baseball and a talent scout for a major league team. I wouldn't trade my job for the world.

Ready to play? You're probably so excited about hitting, running and catching that you want to get started right away. Although your body is pretty flexible, it can still suffer muscle strains, pulls and other injuries. To avoid this, it's important to always perform proper stretching and warm-up exercises before playing.

Begin with a light jog to get your blood flowing faster. If you're playing on a baseball diamond, jog from foul pole to foul pole. Once you're finished, begin stretching your feet and work your way up, stretching your arms and shoulders last. (This will help to leave them loose for the throwing part of your warm-up exercises.) As you stretch, think about the body part that you're working and and how it's used when playing. For example, while stretching the Achilles tendon, ask yourself why it's important (for running, pitching and hitting). If you're not sure why you're stretching a particular muscle, ask your coach to explain.

Individual Stretches

Have you ever gone to a major league game and arrived early? As you take your seat in the stands, you'll probably notice players on the field. Watch what they're doing. The right fielder is running wind sprints, the shortstop is touching his toes and the catcher is doing his best imitation of an ostritch. It might look a little odd and disorganized, but it's not. These guys are stretching—a key part of any pre-game routine.

There are countless ways to stretch the human body. Here's a quick look some of the stretches that baseball players use most. They are all easy and effective.

Figure 3.1

Ankle Rotations

Raise your left foot and point your toes toward the ground. Slowly rotate your ankle in a clockwise direction. (Figure 3.1) Repeat this movement 10 times. Once complete, rotate the same ankle in a counterclockwise direction. Repeat this movement 10 times. Repeat the entire exercise with your right foot.

Figure 3.2

Bent Knee Stretch

Bend your legs slightly at the knees. Touch your toes with your fingers and hold this position for 10 seconds. (Figure 3.2) Rest for five seconds and repeat.

Quadricep Stretch

Grab your ankle and bend your leg at the knee until your foot is touching your rear end. (Figure 3.3) Hold this position for 10 seconds (you should be able to feel the stretch in your thigh muscle.) Repeat with your other leg.

Figure 3.3

Seated Toe Reach

Sit on a flat surface with your legs stretched out in front of you. Spread your legs into a V-shape. With your right arm, reach for the toes on your right foot. (Figure 3.4) Hold the stretch for 10 seconds, then repeat, using your left arm and your right foot.

Figure 3.4

Lower Back Stretch

Sit on a flat surface with your legs stretched out in front of you. Bend your right knee and bring your leg as close to your body as you can, keeping your foot flat on the ground. Place your left elbow against your right knee and turn your body to the right, pushing gently against your knee for 10 seconds. (Figure 3.5) Repeat the exercise with your other knee.

Figure 3.5

Neck Stretch

Stand with your legs shoulder width apart. Gently tilt your head toward your right shoulder. (Figure 3.6) Hold the position for 10 seconds. Repeat the exercise on your left side. (Figure 3.7)

Figure 3.6

Figure 3.7

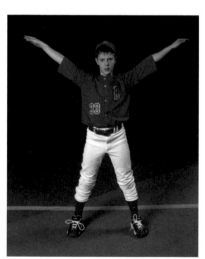

Arm Circles

Moving from your shoulder joint, gently rotate both of arms forward in small, circular motions. Gradually increase the size of the circle. (Figure 3.8) Do this for about 10 seconds, then repeat the exercise using backward circular motions. (Figure 3.9)

Figure 3.8

Figure 3.9

Forearm Stretch

Extend your right arm in front of your body with your palm facing up (Figure 3.10). Using your left hand, slowly pull back the fingers on your right hand. Hold this position for 10 seconds. Repeat the exercise with your left arm. Then, repeat the entire exercise with your palms facing down. (Figure 3.11)

Figure 3.10

Figure 3.11

Figure 3.12

Shoulder Stretch

Stretch your right arm across your chest and hold it with your left arm for 10 seconds. (Figure 3.12) Repeat the exercise with your left arm.

Figure 3.13

Side Bend

Stand with your legs shoulder width apart. Lean down your right side as far as you can go. (Figure 3.13) Hold the position for 10 seconds. Repeat the exercise on your left side.

Team Stretches

Stretching can be a good way for a team to bond before a game or practice. Major league teams do it, and so should you. In fact, stretching as a team should be the first thing you do once all team members are on the field. Don't be the person that holds everyone else up: make sure you know *before* your games or practices what time you need to be at the field and what time stretching begins.

Team stretches can be done in a circle or in lines. The coach and her assistants will stand where all team members can see, leading the stretches in voices loud enough to hear. It's okay to have a bit of fun during the team stretches— you may even be encouraged to talk to your teammates— but don't forget to listen to your coach. This is a great opportunity to learn more about how your body works and how to improve your performance on the field.

Popular team stretching activities include jumping jacks, sprints or anything where counting out loud is an option—it can help motivate you to play. (This comes in handy if you're a little tired when you show up at the park!) Your coach may also ask you to repeat out loud as a group the name of the body part that you are stretching. This will help you focus on what you are doing.

Figure 3.14

Figure 3.15

Figure 3.16

Wind Sprints

Once your stretching is complete, your coach may ask you to run a few wind sprints to get your legs loose. You and your teammates will be instructed to form orderly lines in the outfield, making sure that there is plenty of room between each player. (Figure 3.14) The first players will be asked to sprint against one another for a short distance. You may be encouraged to take a "lead," (by taking a few steps forward), as if you were on base. After checking that you lead is appropriate, your coach will probably ask you to run as fast as you can. (Figure 3.15) Who has more energy today? You or the player two lines down?

Playing Catch

Now it's time to pick up your glove and pair off with a partner for a game of catch. (Figure 3.16) Lightly tossing the ball back and forth will help loosen your arm and prepare you for the game or practice ahead. As you throw, concentrate on your body. If you feel any pain or tension, let your coach know right away. If you are hurt, playing could make the injury worse.

Playing catch is one of the most important components of baseball, yet some young players make mistakes that can lead to the development of poor habits. Played properly, catch can help you improve your skills in several different areas, including arm strength, accuracy, throwing mechanics and hand-to-eye coordination. Whether you're a catcher, a pitcher, an infielder or an outfielder, you need to play catch regularly to improve these skill areas. Major league players do it almost every day; so should you.

Remember that you don't have to be at the ballpark with your teammates to practice this skill. You can play at the park with your next-door neighbor; during recess with your friend; or even in your backyard with your mom or dad. An older brother or sister who also plays baseball might be able to pass on some helpful hints.

Throwing

A proper grip is the key to a good throw. If your hand is big enough to comfortably hold the ball, a cross-seam grip is recommended. Place the pads of your index and middle fingers across the seams of the ball (look for the place on the ball where there is the most space between the seams). Your thumb should be on the underside of the ball, resting in a position between your two fingers. Don't hold the ball deep in your grip—try to keep a space roughly the width of your finger between the ball and your palm. If your hands are smaller, try a three-finger cross-seam grip instead.

When you're ready to play, find a partner and put some distance between each other. You want to be far enough away to make a good throw, but close enough so that you can play without bouncing the ball.

Kneeling Catch

A game of kneeling catch gets you started at the most basic level. Since you don't have to worry about your leg position or your arm action, you are free to concentrate on your grip, wrist action and follow-through.

For this exercise, both you and your partner should go down on one knee. If you throw with your right hand, your right knee should be on the ground; if you're a lefty, put your left knee down.

1. Place the ball in your throwing hand and place your glove hand underneath your throwing elbow.
2. Raise your throwing arm in an L-shape until the elbow

Figure 4.1

Figure 4.2

Figure 4.3

is parallel to or above your throwing shoulder. (Figure 4.1)

3. Focus your eyes on your partner's glove.

4. Release the ball with a flick of your wrist. The ball should be slightly in front of your elbow on release, and your fingers should be on top of the ball. (Figure 4.2)

5. When the ball is returned to you, catch it by closing your glove around it and using your throwing hand to cover the front of the glove. (Figure 4.3)

6. Repeat this process 10 to 15 times.

The Throwing Motion

Once you are comfortable playing catch on your knees, you can begin playing in an upright position and concentrating on completing your throwing motion.

1. Face your partner with your throwing hand holding the ball inside your glove. Hold both hands close to your body immediately in front of your chest. (Figure 4.4)

2. Separate your hands slowly, keeping your thumbs down and bringing your body into a good T position. (Figure 4.5)

3. Throw the ball to your partner, releasing it when your arm passes just in front of your cap.

4. Follow through by bringing your throwing arm down past the lead knee of your glove-arm side.

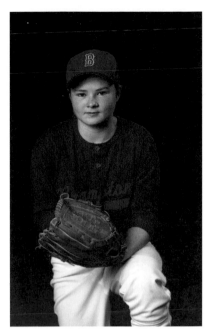

Figure 4.4

Figure 4.5

Stationary Catch

This drill emphasizes the use of your body and your arms. It also focuses on the timing of your release. To prepare, you and your partner should each stand up from your Kneeling Catch positions and take three to five steps back, placing your feet slightly wider than shoulder width apart. Do not move your feet during this exercise.

1. Place the ball in your throwing hand and place your throwing hand in your glove (Figure 4.6).

Figure 4.6

Figure 4.7

2. Remove your throwing hand from your glove and begin a throwing action by pointing the ball toward the ground. Make sure your thumb is pointing down.

3. Swing your arm back in a circular motion, keeping your fingers on top of the ball as much as possible.

4. Point your glove hand and shoulder toward your partner. (Figure 4.7)

5. Continue the circular action with your throwing arm until the ball is ready to be released (shortly after your arm swings past your shoulder and in front of your cap). (Figure 4.8)

6. Follow through with your throwing arm, extending it toward your target and

Figure 4.8

Figure 4.9

fully completing the arc. (Figure 4.9)

7. Repeat this process 10 to 15 times.

Stepping Catch

Now you are ready to use your legs along with the rest of your body. This will give your throwing action more strength, speed and power. Before throwing, you and your partner should each take another three to five steps back.

1. With the ball still in your glove, take one step toward your partner with your throwing-side leg, rotating your foot to the outside by 45 degrees. (Figure 4.10)

2. Remove the ball from your glove with your throwing hand and begin the throwing action described in the Stationary Catch exercise.

3. As the throwing action is taking place, move your glove-side leg toward your partner. (Figure 4.11)

4. Point your glove shoulder, hip and hand toward your partner.

5. Release the ball at approximately the same time as your glove-side leg lands.

6. Follow through with your throwing arm, bringing it down and past your glove-side hip. (Figure 4.12)

Figure 4.10

Figure 4.11

Figure 4.12

Releasing the Ball

When it comes to releasing the ball, there are a number of positions that can be used. The most common is the ¾ arm angle.

The ¾ Arm Angle

1. Raise your throwing arm until it is extended in a straight line from your shoulder.
2. Bend your elbow until your forearm is at a 45-degree angle to the rest of your arm, creating an L-shape. (Figure 4.13)

You'll often hear coaches and other players talk about an upper ¾ release and a lower ¾ release. Both of these positions are achieved by starting with the basic ¾ arm angle. For the overhand throw raise your throwing arm so that it is slightly higher than shoulder level (your elbow should be at roughly the same height as your ear) (Figure 4.14); in the lower ¾ release, you drop your arm a little toward your waist. (Figure 4.15)

Figure 4.13

Figure 4.14

Infielders and pitchers often use the basic ¾ release position. Pitchers also use the overhand release point, as do outfielders. When the ball is released using this angle, it tends to straighten out, making it ideal for outfielders who are throwing to cut-off players or base players.

A Word of Caution

The ¾ arm slot is the best release point for young players—the arm is in a good L-position, the release point is natural and the chances of injury are reduced. With the lower ¾, side arm and underarm release points, your elbow is positioned below the throwing shoulder, potentially putting more strain on the shoulder. Although the ball tends to sink and move more from these release points—making them popular with aspiring pitchers—I highly recommend using the ¾ release point until you are much older and your body and muscles are more fully developed.

Figure 4.15

Receiving

Catching the ball—or receiving—is harder than it looks, especially when you consider that lots of people are scared of the ball when they begin playing. As with all baseball skills, your receiving abilities can be learned and improved over time.

How you receive the ball with your glove depends on where the ball is thrown. If the ball reaches you above the waist, your glove palm and fingers should be facing up, with your fingers pointing toward the ball. If the ball is below the waist, catch it with the fingers of your glove pointing toward the ground.

Whenever the ball is thrown at you, try to use two hands to make the catch as often as possible. Once the ball is in your glove, close the glove and cover the opening with your throwing hand. This way, if the ball takes a bad bounce off the palm of your glove, your throwing hand will prevent it from popping out.

Head and Shoulders

This is a good drill for practicing accurate throwing, catching, judging of the ball and reacting. It's a lot of fun, too. (If you're just starting out, use a tennis ball or a soft rubber ball for this exercise.) Try to throw the ball at the level of your partner's head. If you succeed, give yourself two points. A ball thrown between the shoulders and above the sternum is worth one point. The game continues until someone gets 15 points—and the winner must win by two.

Soft Hands

You and your partner can begin the drill either standing up or in the Kneeling Catch position—with one knee on the ground. You do not need a glove. You can also perform this drill in a standing position.

1. Toss the ball to your partner using an underhand throw. He should catch the ball gently with two hands and bring it up to his chest. He can then return the ball to you. Make sure to catch it the same way. Repeat this exercise 10 times. (Figures 4.16 and 4.17)

2. Repeat the exercise using and overhand throw from your wrist. The ball should be received in the same manner. Repeat this exercise 10 times.

3. Move back approximately three steps and put on your gloves. Repeat the exercise in your new position.

Figure 4.16

Forehand and Backhand

1. Stand facing your partner. You should be far enough away to make a good throw, but close enough so that you don't have to bounce the ball.
2. Throw the ball to your partner so that he has to make a one-handed forehand catch (slightly in front of his body). He should return the ball to you in the same way. Repeat this exercise 5 times.
3. Then, throw the ball to your partner so that he has to make a one-handed backhand catch (slightly behind his body). Repeat 5 times.
4. Repeat the entire exercise again, beginning with forehand and ending with backhand.

Figure 4.17

5/Infielding

The infield consists of four positions: the first baseman, second baseman, third baseman and shortstop. Although all must share the responsibility for turning infield hits into outs, each position is unique.

The first baseman needs good hands—he'll be fielding a lot of ground balls, and will often have to "scoop" errant throws out of the dirt. The second baseman needs enough speed and agility to make plays on the fly, sometimes with the baserunner moving toward him. The shortstop should have the most range. He covers balls hit "in the hole" (anything beyond the reach of the third baseman) as well as behind second base. He is often the key to successful double plays. The third baseman must rely on his reflexes (right-handed batters often drill balls toward third) and his strong throwing arm; a throw from third has a long way to travel before reaching first base.

Whatever position you play, the ability to field ground balls is crucial. Most pitchers are taught to keep the ball low and to force the batter to hit the ball on the ground. In this chapter, we will focus on the proper fielding techniques for balls hit on the ground.

Fielding Ground Balls

To properly field a ground ball, you need to be in the correct position when the batter comes to the plate and when the pitch is thrown. A good catch comes next, followed by an accurate throw to your target.

The Rest Position

The rest position is taken when you are waiting for the pitcher to throw the ball to the plate.

1. Rest your hands on your knees and crouch with your weight shifted onto the balls of your feet. (Figure 5.1)
2. Position your feet so that they are slightly wider than shoulder width apart.

The Ready Position

Once the pitcher begins his delivery to the plate, position yourself so that you are pre-pared to field a ball that is hit toward you.

1. Lower your arms toward the ground in front of your feet.
2. Bend your knees and slightly lower your rear end toward the ground. (Figure 5.2)

This last point is important. Fielding a ball is easier when you are moving upward from the ground. Some players even choose to place their gloves directly on the ground when in the ready position.

Fielding the Ball

Once the ball is hit toward you, you need to begin your fielding motion.

1. As the ball approaches, take two or three steps toward it. This is called charging the ball. (Figure 5.3)
2. Place your glove hand on the ground, with your fingers pointing down and your hand relaxed.

Figure 5.1

Figure 5.2

Figure 5.3

3. Keep your glove in front of your body whenever possible. This is called surrounding the ball. If the ball takes a bad hop, it will drop to the ground in front of you. If you field the ball between your legs, a bad hop can role away, allowing the baserunner to advance.

4. As the ball approaches, use your throwing hand to cover the top of the ball and to assist with closing the glove once the ball is inside. (Figure 5.4)

Figure 5.4

Making the Out

Once a routine ground ball has been fielded, you must complete the play by either making an accurate throw to a teammate, or by tagging the running out at the base. By fielding the ball in front of your body and slightly toward your throwing-arm side, you will ease the transition from fielding to throwing.

Throwing the Runner Out

1. Grip the ball with two fingers crossing the seams and relax your hand.
2. Throw from the $3/4$ arm angle if possible. (Variations in your grip or arm angle could cause movement on your throw, making it more difficult to catch.)
3. Whenever possible, position your front shoulder, hip and foot so that they are moving toward your target.

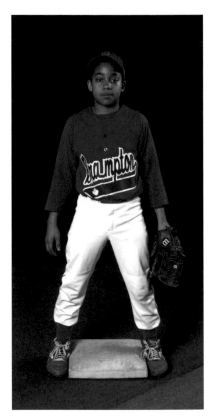

Figure 5.5

Figure 5.6

Tagging the Runner Out

1. Straddle the base with both feet, making sure that you have a clear view of the ball. (Figure 5.5)
2. Receive the ball with two hands. (Figure 5.6)
3. Make the tag using your glove hand only (younger players may need to keep their throwing hand on the ball during the tag).
4. Sweep the glove in front of the base. (Figure 5.7)
5. Remove the glove once the baserunner has made contact.

Figure 5.7

Ready for Anything

It would be nice if every ball that you had to catch was hit directly to you, but that's not likely to happen. Infielders have to be ready to face all sorts of hits—from slow rollers to hard smashes. Here's a look at how to field some of the most common hits.

Hard Smashes

Staying low to the ground and in front of the ball is essential in any play, and that includes the hard smash—a ball that comes off the bat so hard that it's impossible to charge, and often impossible to catch (unless its moving right toward you). Hard smashes are more likely to reach the corner infielders (who are located closest to home plate), giving them very little time to react. If you're playing one of these positions, your main job is to not let the ball get past you. One way to do this is to position your glove-side knee and your glove on the ground. This will reduce the space between your legs and increase your chances of blocking the ball.

Slow Rollers

A soft hit—or a slow roller—may seem like an easy out,

Figure 5.8

Figure 5.9

but a successful play requires great anticipation and speed.

1. Get to the ball as quickly as possible.
2. Step forward with your glove-side foot as the ball reaches your glove. (Figure 5.8)
3. Transfer the ball quickly into your throwing hand, step onto your throwing-side leg and throw the ball, using a lower $3/4$ release position. (Figures 5.9 and 5.10)

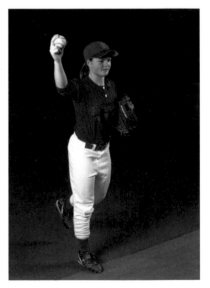

Figure 5.10

Side to Side

On a ball hit sharply to the left or right, the infielder's first priority is to make a safe catch. When the ball is hit, try to react quickly enough to get in front of it.

1. Pivot on the foot that is closest to the ball. Cross over with your opposite foot and begin a running stride. (Figure 5.11)
2. As the hitter runs toward first, relax your glove-side arm and keep your glove low to the ground.
3. Catch the ball and take two or three steps to align yourself with your target. (Figure 5.12)
4. Set your feet into a proper throwing position and release the ball.

Figure 5.11

Figure 5.12

Depending on the play, you might not have time to properly align yourself and set your feet. Although you always want to make the throw as soon as possible, be sure that you've got a good grip on the ball. A good grip is the key to a good throw. A bad throw could miss its mark, allowing the baserunner to advance.

Infielding Drills

Ground Balls

1. Have a partner roll a ball to you along the ground.
2. As you receive the ball, get into a good throwing position.
3. Make a short throw to your partner.

As you improve, ask your partner to increase the speed of the rolls until you can successfully field a ball hit from a bat.

Pick-Ups

1. Have your partner roll a ball to either your left or right side.
2. Use a shuffling step to get into fielding position.
3. Receive the ball and toss it to your partner.
4. Repeat this exercise 5 times, alternating sides.

Cross-Overs

1. Have your partner say "go" and give you a hand signal to run in a particular direction.
2. Pivot or step in that direction, cross over with your

Figure 5.13

other foot and run several steps before slowing down as if you were going to field a ball.

3. Simulate the fielding and throwing actions.

4. When you are comfortable with your steps and your speed, repeat the exercise using a ball.

Wall Drill

1. Throw a soft ball against a gymnasium wall or a brick wall.

2. Field the ball as it bounces back to you.

3. Gradually increase the speed of your throws.

Quick Hands

This drill is especially useful for middle infielders. It will help you learn how to quickly get rid of the ball. (Figure 5.13)

1. Stand facing your partner at a distance of approximately 20 feet (6 m).

2. Have your partner throw the ball to you so that you catch it at chest level.

3. Make the catch, quickly transfer the ball from your glove to your throwing hand, and return the ball to your partner.

4. Repeat this exercise 10 times, trying to improve your speed. (Have someone use a stopwatch to time you, if possible.)

Turn Around

This drill is designed to improve foot quickness, reflexes, and hand-to-eye coordination.

1. Stand facing your partner at a distance of approximately 20 feet (6 m).

2. Turn around so that your back is to your partner.

3. Have your partner signal the start of the drill by saying, "go."

4. When your hear the signal, turn around as quickly as you can.

5. As soon as you turn around, your partner will roll a ground ball to you, varying the location from left to right to straight on. Field the ball and return it to your partner.

6. Repeat this exercise 5 times.

6/Outfielding

The outfield is made up of the right fielder, the center fielder and the left fielder. As with the infield, each position requires a unique set of skills and abilities. The right fielder, for example, should have the strongest arm. The throw from right field to third base is the longest throw an outfielder will have to make—and with home plate just ninety feet from third, it can be a key play during any game. Like the shortstop, the center fielder covers the most ground. Speed is essential, as is the ability to read the ball well as it's coming off the bat. The left fielder should possess some speed and have an accurate throwing arm.

Catching in the Outfield

Although the ground covered is greater than in the infield, playing the outfield requires the same fielding skills. A good rest-ready position and the ability to judge the ball as it comes off the bat can help you get a jump on both ground and fly balls.

Judging the Ball

The height, sound and direction of a ball as it comes off the bat are the strongest indicators of where it's headed. A loud "ping" off an aluminum bat or a "crack" off a wooden bat often means that the ball has been hit hard. After making note of the sound, watch the flight and speed of the ball. If it's moving quickly, back up and prepare to field. If the ball has been hit high, watch as the ball arcs and hits its highest point. With practice, you'll be able to determine roughly where the ball will come down.

When a ball is hit in the air, always be prepared to turn your body toward it. For example, if you're playing right field and the ball comes off the bat to the left, be prepared to pivot left. Do not guess where the ball is going to be hit. An error in judgment may give the runner an extra base or two.

Figure 6.1

The Rest Position

1. Stand in a relaxed upright position.
2. Position your feet so that they are shoulder width apart, with one slightly in front of the other.
3. Balance your weight evenly on the balls of your feet. (Figure 6.1)

The Ready Position

Once the pitcher begins her delivery, you can move into the ready position. (Figure 6.2)

1. Shift your weight toward the balls of your feet.
2. Bend your knees slightly.
3. Stay alert—you need to react to balls off of the bat.

Figure 6.2

Footwork

Footwork is important in getting a good jump on the ball. Taking the right steps will allow you to get to the ball quickly and effectively.

1. Pivot on the foot nearest the ball.
2. Cross over with your opposite foot. (Figure 6.3)

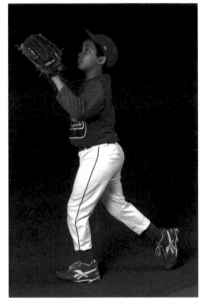

Figure 6.3

3. Run aggressively to the ball.

Always run on the balls of your feet to prevent your head from bouncing. (This can interfere with how clearly you see the ball.)

Calling For It

If you believe you can make a clean catch, call for it: "I got it!" If another player calls for the ball at the same time, remember that the center fielder has priority over the other players. (Figures 6.4, 6.5, and 6.6.)

If another player has waved you off the play, say "take it" and get out of the way.

Figure 6.4

Figure 6.5

Figure 6.6

Catching Fly Balls

Outfielders often have to track down fly balls. Judging the ball, taking the correct route to the ball, communicating with your teammates, and catching the ball properly all come into play.

1. Stay underneath the ball (some players like to think of their forehead as a magnet that attracts the ball). (Figure 6.7)
2. Move slightly toward your throwing-arm side just before the ball lands in your glove. (Figure 6.8)
3. Catch the ball at head level on your throwing side. (Figure 6.9)
4. Cover the opening of your glove with your throwing hand.

Catching Ground Balls

If you play the outfield, you probably won't have to catch as many ground balls as your infield teammates, but you should still know the drill.

1. Keep the ball in front of your body.
2. Charge the ball if possible (Always take the quickest route. A good angle will allow you to cut off a ball in the gap and create an alignment with your target.)

Figure 6.7

Figure 6.8

Figure 6.9

Throwing from the Outfield

Outfielders should try to throw from an overhand release point. A lower release point may cause the ball to sink or tail (move laterally), making it more difficult to catch.

The Cut-Off Person

Your throw should always be to your cut-off person, or relay. For example, if you are playing a ball down the line or in the gap, there should be a relay person—usually an infielder—raising her arms and looking toward you. If your team is well prepared, you'll know in advance who the cut-off person is for different plays. (Figure 6.10) Throw the ball at head level. If it is a good throw, the cut-off person may let it go directly to its target. If not, she will catch it and relay it to the next base.

Don't worry if your throw to a base is low. It may bounce, but it will be easier to catch than a high throw. It will probably be more accurate, too. High throws—especially those that are overthrown—may miss their mark, allowing the runners to advance.

Figure 6.10

Figure 6.11

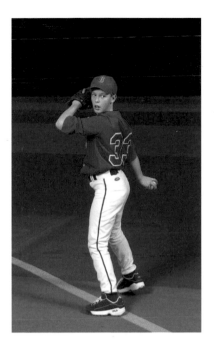

Figure 6.12

Figure 6.13

The Crow Hop

The "crow hop" is a term that describes the lower body and foot movement used when making a throw from a fielding position. It's frequently used by outfielders.

1. Step forward with your fielding-side foot.
2. Once the ball is fielded hop on your back foot. (Figure 6.11)
3. As you land on your back foot, transfer the ball from your glove to throwing hand, and begin your throwing motion. (Figure 6.12)
4. Release the ball from an overhand position and follow through. (Figure 6.13)

Outfielding Drills

Fly Balls

1. Have your partner throw a ball in the air.
2. Position yourself underneath the ball and try to make the catch. (Figure 6.14)
3. When you can successfully catch thrown balls, have your partner hit off a bat instead.

Figure 6.14

Communication

1. Choose two partners—one to catch balls with you and one to bat.
2. Have the batting partner hit balls in the air.
3. Practice calling for the ball with your catching partner. Whoever calls "I got it" first gets to make the catch. (Figure 6.15)

Figure 6.15

Route Running

1. Have your partner hit a series of ground balls in different directions.
2. Practice judging where the ball will go, receiving the ball and throwing to the infield.

Relay

The relay drill is designed to improve hand quickness and throwing accuracy. It is particularly useful for outfielders making throws to cut-off players. If you are practicing in groups, see which is faster.

1. Line up a minimum of four players at equal distance from one another.
2. Have the first player throw the ball to second player. (Each receiving player should have his hands in the air, acting as the cut-off player.) (Figure 6.16)

Figure 6.16

3. The receiving player should catch the ball, turn around quickly and throw to the next person in line.
4. Keep the ball going to the end of the line; then, repeat the exercise in reverse.

7/Pitching

Pitching can be one of the most rewarding positions in baseball. Unlike other players on the field, the pitcher is involved in every single play of the game. In the major leagues, pitchers can throw more than 100 pitches over the course of a game—each one carefully chosen based on the batter, the count, the number of outs and whether or not there are runners on base.

The decision about what pitch to throw is made by the pitcher and the catcher, who communicate through a series of signs—hand signals that the catcher delivers from behind the plate. The pitcher agrees or disagrees with the call by nodding or shaking his head. Before the game begins, make sure that you and your catcher agree on what sign refers to what pitch. It's also a good idea to have a back-up set of signs just in case.

As a pitcher, your main job is to throw strikes—and to throw them consistently. The problem is that batters try to hit balls thrown in the strike zone. In order to be effective, you have to change the hitters' timing, making them swing too early or too late. Speed, movement, accuracy, mechanics and good instincts all play a role. So does practice.

The ability to throw hard is a natural gift, but good pitchers can improve their velocity and control by using the correct mechanics. Although many pitchers want to throw a variety of pitches, a fastball and a change-up are all you'll need at first.

The Fastball

A good fastball is the result of proper mechanics and a smooth, rhythmic delivery. It has good velocity and good movement. This movement—such as sinking or tailing—is the result of various spins put on the ball at release.

The fastball is the most important pitch in baseball. When starting out, pitchers are encouraged to use their fastball at least 75 percent of the time. If you have a good one, you will be able to intimidate hitters—especially if you can throw it where you want. Pitching legends such as Roger Clemens, Randy Johnson and Curt Schilling regularly reach speeds of 95 miles per hour with their fastballs, but they'll still struggle through a game if they can't hit the strike zone.

There are two basic fastball grips—the four-seam and the two-seam.

The Four-Seam Fastball
The four-seam fastball uses the most basic grip. It results in a faster, straighter pitch than the two-seam grip.

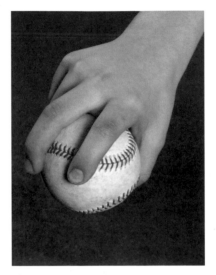

Figure 7.1

1. Place your middle and index fingers *across* the seams that are closest together. (Figure 7.1)
2. Place your thumb underneath the ball.
3. Hold the ball comfortably toward the end of your fingers, not choked back in the palm of your hand.
4. Keep your fingers close together. While wider spacing may lead to better comfort it will lessen the movement of your pitch, as well as decreasing velocity and accuracy.

The Two-Seam Fastball
The two-seam fastball has more movement and slightly less velocity than the four-seam throw. It is often used when a pitcher wants a ball hit on the ground.

1. Place your middle and index fingers *along* the two seams that are closest together. (Figure 7.2)
2. Place your thumb underneath the ball.
3. Grip the ball, applying slightly more pressure to your middle finger.
4. Hold the ball comfortably toward the end of your fingers, not choked back in the palm of your hand.

Figure 7.2

The Change-Up

Once you are able to locate your fastball consistently for strikes, a good second pitch to learn is the change-up. The purpose of a change-up is to upset the hitter's timing and force her to be off-balance.

The key to throwing a good change-up is to use the same arm speed that is used when throwing a fastball while also reducing the velocity of the ball. Over at home plate, the hitter will interpret your motion as a fastball delivery. He'll either swing too soon or be completely fooled and not swing at all.

The arm action required for the change-up is similar to the fastball (see Delivery and Mechanics, page 80), but the pitch uses a different grip. Like the fastball, the change-up can be thrown using either a two-seam or four-seam grip. Experiment with both until you know what works best for you. A pitch may feel comfortable in your hand, but if you're having a difficult time locating it for strikes, alterations to the grip might be required.

The Four-Seam Change-Up

Similar to the four-seam fastball, this pitch is the straightest of the two change-ups.

1. Spread out your index, middle and ring fingers and position them so that they *cross* the ball's seams. (Figure 7.3)
2. Place your thumb and pinkie finger on the bottom third of the ball.
3. Grip the ball lightly against your palm.
4. Keep your wrist stiff, or locked, with no downward snap and point your fingers up on release.

The Two-Seam Change-Up

The two-seam change-up requires a similar positioning of the fingers on the ball, except the fingers are not lying across the seams, but *along* them (like the two-seam fastball). (Figure 7.4) This pitch will have a sinking action and a loose rotation.

Figure 7.3

Figure 7.4

Delivery and Mechanics

Once you are comfortable with the various pitching grips, it's time to learn proper delivery. Good delivery will improve your accuracy and velocity, and minimize your risk of injury.

The Delivery

1. Stand on the mound near the middle of the rubber. Put both feet on the rubber and keep your eyes on the target. (If you're a righty, you may stand slightly to your right side, and vice versa if you're a lefty.) (Figure 7.5)

2. Look to the catcher for the sign (Figure 7.6) and take a small step back with your stride foot (left foot for right-handers, right foot for lefties). Your stride foot should land at a slight angle to the rubber. (Figure 7.7)

3. Pivot your other foot so that it is parallel to the rubber. Your heel should be touching the rubber.

4. As your pivot foot goes into place, lift your striding knee toward your chest, keeping your knee and foot relaxed and toes pointing down. (Figure 7.8)

5. As your stride leg begins to move towards the plate, remove the ball from your glove and begin your throwing action, keeping your fingers on top of the ball. (Figure 7.9)

6. Point your glove-side arm toward the catcher's mitt. (Figure 7.10)

7. Stride toward the target, landing on the front part of your stride foot in a slightly closed position (toe pointing to 10 o'clock).

8. As your stride leg lands, your throwing arm should be coming through and releasing the ball. The ball should leave your hand when your arm is near the tip of your hat. (Figure 7.11)

Figure 7.5

Figure 7.6

Figure 7.7

Figure 7.8

Figure 7.9

Figure 7.10

Figure 7.11

Figure 7.12

Figure 7.13

9. Follow through with the throwing arm, continuing a downward movement past your glove-side hip. (Figure 7.12)
10. Position yourself to field a ground ball. (Figure 7.13)

The Set Position

If there are runners on base, a pitcher should always assume the set position before throwing. This position will allow him to deliver the ball to either home plate or an occupied base.

1. Stand with your back facing first base (righties) or third base (lefties).
2. Position your feet so that they are parallel to one another and approximately shoulder width apart.
3. Place the outside of your pivot foot against the front edge of the rubber.
4. Bring your hands together in the area between your chest and your belly button.

Pitching Drills

All pitchers need to understand the importance of arm care. Never throw when your arm is sore, and always complete a proper warm-up.

Warm-Up
1. Run from the right field foul pole to the left field foul pole and back. Repeat.
2. Stretch.
3. Complete two 90-foot (27 m) wind sprints at about 75 percent of your maximum speed.
4. Play catch with a partner until your arm is loose.

Balance Point
The goal of this drill is to create and maintain balance over the pitching rubber.

1. Stand on the mound with your feet together and your hands together at chest level.
2. Lift your stride leg straight up. (Figure 7.14)
3. Hold this position for three seconds. (Figure 7.15)
4. As you develop better balance, have a partner toss a ball to you as you are lifting your leg.

Figure 7.14

Figure 7.15

Hand Separation

This drill helps develop the proper timing of your hand break—baseball talk for taking the ball out of your glove and beginning your throwing motion.

1. Get into the set position.
2. Position your lead leg in a stride position and keep your hands together. (Figure 7.16)
3. Separate your hands (thumbs to thighs) as your stride leg goes forward. (Figure 7.17)
4. Release the ball and follow through. (Figures 7.18 and Figure 7.19)

Balanced Landing

1. On a flat surface, assume a proper landing position (with the toe of your landing foot pointing in).
2. Deliver the ball to a partner 15 to 30 feet (4.5–9 m) away by shifting your weight onto your back foot and rotating your pivot foot.
3. Follow through, maintaining your balance over your stride-leg foot.
4. Receive a throw from your partner.

Figure 7.16

Figure 7.17

Figure 7.18

Figure 7.19

8/Catching

Catching is the most physically demanding position in baseball.

Catchers squat behind the plate for the entire game, sometimes catching as many as 150 pitches. They block pitches thrown in the dirt, get hit by pitches and foul tips, block plays at the plate and throw runners out. Along with the pitcher, the catcher "calls" the game, deciding which pitches will be thrown to which batters. They also have to take their own turns at bat.

Successful catchers will tell you that the position takes lots of hard work. When the hard work pays off, though, it's a lot of fun.

The Equipment

Since catchers are likely to get more than a few bumps and bruises, the proper equipment is essential. Here are a few tips:

- Your mask, skullcap and throat protector should fit comfortably and loosely so that they can be taken off quickly during a game. Some catchers prefer a goalie-style mask, which also works well.
- Your chest protector should be comfortable and well fitted—not too tight and not too loose—especially around the neck.
- Your shin guards must provide full coverage of the feet, shins and knees. Extra padding over the side or on top of the knees is a bonus.
- Your shin guards should fasten on the outside so that they do not clip together when you run.
- Your glove should be of an appropriate size and comfortable on your hand. (A catcher's glove is larger than a regular fielding glove and should have extra padding to protect your hand against high-speed pitches.)

Proper catching equipment is the key to avoiding injury. In this picture, the player's mask and glove are fine, but the chest protector is too loose around the neck and the knee pads are too big—they should sit on the knees, not mid-thigh.

- An athletic supporter and cup should always be worn.

Preparing to Catch

Before the ball is thrown, you and your pitcher must agree on both pitch and placement. In order to do this, you'll need to communicate through signs. Once the sign is accepted, you're ready to receive the ball.

Giving the Sign

1. When giving a sign to the pitcher, you should be in an upright crouch, with your weight on your toes and your glove on your knee. (Figure 8.1)
2. Deliver the sign from between your legs.

Getting Ready

1. After the sign is accepted, slowly move toward the area where you expect the ball to cross the plate. (Don't move too early, or you may tip off the batter about the pitch you're expecting.)
2. Get as close to the plate as possible without interfering with the hitter—an arm's length behind the batter is good.
3. Position your body so that you're facing square to the pitcher.
4. Distribute your weight evenly on the balls of your feet.
5. Keep your back straight and your thighs parallel to the ground. (Figure 8.2)
6. As the pitcher starts her throwing motion, extend your glove hand toward the mound, keeping your arm slightly bent. (Figure 8.3)
7. Hold your glove hand at a slight angle, with the face exposed to the pitcher.
8. Position your glove hand behind the middle of the plate, level with the player's knees. If the target is higher, position the glove accordingly.

Figure 8.1

Figure 8.2

Figure 8.3

Making the Catch

How you catch the ball can help you get the call that you want—"Strike!" Proper technique will also lessen

Figure 8.4

the strain on your catching hand.

1. Catch the ball with your arm slightly extended and glove hand relaxed.
2. Move back slightly once you receive the pitch, allowing your glove to give a little. (Figure 8.4)
3. Follow the ball all the way into the glove with your eyes. Do not blink, especially during the swing.
4. Move as little as possible when making the catch.

Catching a Pop-Up
While fly balls—or pop-ups—

are often the responsibility of infielders and outfielders, catchers will also face them from time to time. Since the ball is often moving backward into foul territory or behind home plate, a good catch requires lots of concentration.

1. Keep your eyes open as the batter swings. Do not blink.
2. Once you see the ball in the air, take off your mask and hold it in your throwing hand. (Figure 8.5)
3. Turn your back to the infield.
4. Move to the area where you

Figure 8.5

Figure 8.6

Figure 8.7

expect to make the catch, keeping the ball in line with your forehead.

5. Toss your mask away from the ball and the plate. (Figure 8.6)

6. Catch the ball with both hands above your forehead. (Figure 8.7)

Blocking the Ball

No matter how hard you try, not all pitches are going to be caught cleanly. If the ball is in the dirt, your first job is to block it, especially if there are runners on base.

1. Drop to both knees with your body square to the ball. (Figure 8.8)

2. Keep your rear end and your hips up.

3. Place both hands between your knees. Relax your bare hand, placing your palm forward and your thumb at the side.

4. Slightly bend both arms and tuck them in toward the side of your body.

5. Tuck your chin toward your chest.

6. Curl your body forward to keep the ball in front of you. (Figure 8.9)

7. Be prepared to jump up after blocking the ball and make a throw to a base.

Figure 8.8

Figure 8.9

Completing the Play

Always be prepared to throw the ball when runners are on base. Even if you don't have the strongest arm on the team, good footwork and a quick release will help get the ball quickly to your target.

Figure 8.10

Figure 8.11

Before you throw, though, be sure that you have a good chance of getting the runner out. If it appears that the runner will be safe, even with an accurate throw, do not make the attempt. If you miss your mark, or the receiving infielder makes an error, the runner could advance by one or two bases.

On all throws from the plate, your arm action should shorten up slightly. Your throwing hand should be higher than your shoulder, and your fingers should be on top of the ball.

Figure 8.12

Figure 8.13

1. Keep your throwing hand in a relaxed fist with the thumb tucked inside. (Figure 8.10)
2. Shift your weight toward the front of your feet and remain in a slightly upright crouch.
3. As you receive the ball,

move upward and forward. (Figure 8.11)
4. Pull your glove in toward your throwing shoulder. (Figure 8.12)
5. Separate your hands and step forward with your glove-side leg. (Figure 8.13)
6. Release the ball. (Figure 8.14)

Figure 8.14

Figure 8.15

Figure 8.16

Figure 8.17

Tagging the Runner

A close play at home plate is one of the most exciting in baseball. A catcher needs to know how to apply the tag correctly so that he can record the out and avoid injury.

1. Always assume the play will be close.
2. Slightly bend your left knee and position it toward the third baseline. Be prepared to give with your left knee. (Figure 8.15)
3. Catch the ball and place it in your throwing hand. Sweep the plate with both hands. (If the runner is not sliding into home, tag the body part that's closest to touching the plate.) (Figures 8.16 and 8.17)

Catching Drills

Figure 8.18

Receiving
1. Assume a proper catching stance.
2. Have your partner kneel 10 to 15 (3–4.5 m) feet away and toss balls to you.
3. Gradually increase the speed of the tosses and the distance from which they are thrown.

Blocking
1. Assume a proper catching stance.
2. Have your partner kneel 10 to 15 feet (3–4.5 m) away and toss balls to you, aiming slightly to the left or the right so that you have to shift position in order to block the throw. (Figure 8.18)
3. Gradually increase the speed of the tosses and the distance from which they are thrown.

Figure 8.19

Block and Recover

1. Place a ball in front of the plate and drop to your knees.
2. Get into a blocking position, recover the ball and assume a throwing position. (Figure 8.19)
3. Repeat the exercise with a partner throwing the ball to you.

Figure 8.20

Throwing Progression

1. In a proper catching position, receive the ball from a partner.
2. Get into a standing position and return the ball to your partner. (Figure 8.20)
3. Gradually increase the distance between you and your partner until you are as far apart as home plate and second base.

If pitching is the most challenging part of playing baseball, hitting might be the most fun. Every player dreams of reaching base each time he comes up to bat, or of hitting the ball over the fence. As with all baseball skills, the more you practice hitting, the more you will improve.

Before discussing the the technical aspects of hitting—the stance and the swing—it's important to learn about bat selection. The right bat will help you achieve comfort and leverage in your swing.

When choosing a bat, pick it up and take a few swings. How does it feel? It should be comfortable in your hands, and it shouldn't be too heavy. Try holding the bat out to your side. If you can keep it raised for a short period of time without difficulty, it's probably the right weight.

Hitting Basics

A proper grip allows you to hold the bat comfortably and take the best possible swing. If you hold the bat too tightly, you won't be able to extend your arms. If your grip is too loose, the bat will feel heavy, making it difficult to swing the barrel through the strike zone.

The Grip

1. Hold the bat handle at the base of your fingers (it shouldn't be sitting in your palm). (Figure 9.1)
2. Use a firm but relaxed grip.
3. Position your hands so that the middle knuckles of your top hand sit between the middle and last knuckles of your bottom hand. (Figure 9.2)
4. Choke up on the bat—by sliding your hands an inch or two above the knob—to increase your control. (Figure 9.3)

Figure 9.1

Figure 9.2

Figure 9.3

Figure 9.4

The Stance

Your stance—or how you stand at the plate—is a key element of successful hitting. It can affect how well you swing the bat and how well you see the pitch. A proper stance will also make it possible to hit a ball on either the inner or outer part of the plate.

1. Stand with your feet approximately shoulder width apart.
2. Position your feet so that both are the same distance away from the plate. This is called an even, or square, stance. (Figure 9.4)
3. Stand with your feet close enough to the plate so that your swing can cover the whole plate.

The Approach

Batters need to prepare both physically and mentally before hitting the ball. A positive frame of mind is important when you step up to the plate, but so is a good position.

1. Look toward the pitcher with both eyes. (Figure 9.5)

Figure 9.5

2. Stand with your feet approximately shoulder width apart.
3. Balance your weight equally on both feet and bend your knees slightly.
4. Raise the bat so that it's even with your back shoulder, holding it at a 45-degree angle. (Figure 9.6)
5. Relax your hands, arms and legs.

The Swing

When the pitch is delivered, make sure that you're ready. Don't be afraid to swing the bat, even if you miss. It never hurts to be aggressive.

1. When the pitcher starts his stride, slowly move your hands back and up into a slightly raised position. (Figure 9.7)

2. As the ball is released, take a short stride toward the pitcher with your front leg.
3. Take a short, quick swing, keeping your front leg strong and pivoting on your back foot. (Figure 9.8)
4. Follow through, completing the swinging motion when your bat comes around to your shoulder. (Figure 9.9)
5. Drop the bat so that it is out of the catcher's way.

Figure 9.8

Figure 9.6

Figure 9.7

Figure 9.9

Bunting

Bunting is designed to make the ball travel a very short distance. Often, bunts are used in "sacrifice" situations—where the batter will sacrifice himself to help a baserunner advance.

Another popular option is to bunt during a "squeeze" play, when a runner is on third. In this case, the goal is to draw the infielder off the bag to make the catch, allowing the runner to come in and score.

1. Position your feet so that they are shoulder width apart.
2. Stand forward in the batter's box with your feet square to the plate.
3. Hold your body in a relaxed position and flex your knees.

4. Keep your arms relaxed and forward.
5. Position your bat in front of the plate at the top of the strike zone. (Figure 9.10) The barrel should be angled so that it points slightly upward from your hands. (Figure 9.11)
6. Hold the bat with a relaxed but firm grip. Your thumb and index finger should make a V, with the thumb on top and fingers underneath. (Figure 9.12)
7. As the pitcher begins his motion, slide your top hand up the barrel. (Move the bat up and down in the strike zone by bending and straightening your knees.) (Figure 9.13)
8. Wait for the ball to enter the strike zone before making contact. Don't jab at the ball. (Figure 9.14)

Figure 9.12

Figure 9.13

Figure 9.10

Figure 9.11

Figure 9.14

Hitting Drills

Shadow Swings

1. Practice swinging at an imaginary ball, focusing on a downward approach.
2. Maintain a proper stance and ready position.
3. Keep your hands back and maintain a strong front side (shoulder, leg and hip).
4. Finish the swing with a good follow-through.

Hitting Tee

1. Place a hitting tee 10 feet from a fence or screen.
2. Assume a proper stance and ready position. (Figure 9.15)
3. Keep your eyes on the ball and your front side strong.
4. Swing, hit the ball and follow through. (Figures 9.16, 9.17, and 9.18)

Figure 9.17

Figure 9.15

Figure 9.16

Figure 9.18

Soft Toss

1. Stand in front of a screen or fence as if you were standing at home plate, ready to bat.
2. Have your partner kneel about 20 feet (6 m) in front of you, off to one side.
3. Have him softly toss a ball (whiffle, tennis or baseball) over home plate. (Figure 9.19)
4. With as level a swing as possible, hit the ball hard into the screen. (Figure 9.20)
5. Repeat this exercise 10 times and then switch places with your partner.

Bunt for Base Hit

1. Stand facing your partner as if he is a pitcher and you are at bat.
2. Have your partner throw the ball (not too hard). Try to bunt into fair territory. (Make sure that you are still in the batter's box when you make contact.)
3. Once you make contact, pivot with your front foot, cross over and begin running. (Figures 9.21 and 9.22)
4. Repeat this exercise 10 times, keeping track of your "base hits." Switch places with your partner.

Whiffle Ball

1. Have your partner throw whiffle balls at you.
2. Swing only at balls that are in the strike zone.
3. Repeat this exercise 10 times and then switch places with your partner.

Figure 9.21

Figure 9.19

Figure 9.20

Figure 9.22

10/Baserunning

Baserunning comes naturally to most players—unfortunately, so does poor technique. Learning to run the bases well will increase your speed and decrease your chances of being injured.

As you run, pump your arms forward and backward, keeping your elbows bent and arms close to your body. Move your hands from your hips (at the back of the arm pump) to shoulder height (at the front). When your foot is off the ground, keep your knee bent and raised in front of your body. Lean forward slightly and stay relaxed.

Getting on Base

You've just hit the ball safely, and you're pretty sure that you've got a single. You'd better hustle, though, or the play at the base could be close! Any ball hit on the ground in the infield will be thrown to first base—make sure you beat that throw. If you manage to hit it past the infielders, the play will probably be at second.

Running On an Infield Hit

1. Pivot on your front foot and step forward with your back foot, following through on your swing. (Drop the bat after your follow-through.)
2. Move your feet quickly and pump your arms hard on the first three steps.
3. Run in a straight line toward first base. (Figure 10.1)
4. Touch the front part of the base with your foot. (Figure 10.2)
5. Run through the base and take a quick look over your right shoulder to see if the ball has been overthrown. (Figure 10.3)
6. Shorten your steps quickly and come to a stop.
7. Turn to the right and walk back to the base.

Figure 10.1

Figure 10.2

Figure 10.3

Figure 10.4

Figure 10.5

Running On an Outfield Hit

1. Start running as soon as you're sure that you've hit safely.
2. Run in an arc toward first base, taking yourself into foul territory. (Figure 10.4)
3. Touch the front inside corner of first base with either foot. Do not break your stride.
4. Round the base and quickly slow to a stop and return to first base (Figure 10.5). Keeping your eyes on the ball.
5. Be ready to continue to second base in the event of an error.
6. If the ball has been fielded cleanly and thrown to second, promptly return to the bag at first.

Getting Past First

You're safe at first. What next? Getting around the bases is the key to making sure your team scores a run; but how do you know when to run, when to steal, how far to lead off or when to stay put? Watch your coach. She should be signaling you from the sidelines. Her advice will depend on the number of outs, the direction of the hit, the strength of the outfielder's arm and your own speed on the bases.

Figure 10.7

Leading Off

You can start to take your lead as soon as the pitcher has stepped off the rubber.

1. Keep both eyes on the pitcher.
2. Lead off the back corner of the base in a straight line toward the next base. (Figure 10.6)
3. Take approximately three small side steps toward the next base. Do not use cross-over steps. (Figure 10.7)
4. Maintain a balanced stance and be ready to move in either direction.
5. Once the ball has been delivered, take two shuffle steps.

Figure 10.6

Sliding In

Any time there is a close play at a base it is important for the runner to slide. Sliding will not only make it easier for you to get to the base without going past it, it will make it more difficult for the baseplayer to tag you out.

Timing a slide can be difficult. You may need to practice in non-competitive situations in order to determine when you should start your slide.

1. Take off from either foot.
2. As you approach the base, bend your take-off leg and slide with one leg bent under the other.
3. Throw both hands back over your head. (Figure 10.8)
4. Lean back slightly and slide on the full length of your bent leg. (Figure 10.9)

Figure 10.8

Figure 10.9

Baserunning Drills

Form Running

1. March in place, making sure to raise your knees high with each step.
2. Run in place, using the same technique.
3. Practice running up and down hills, using the same technique.

Baserunning

1. Run as fast as you can from home to first. (Figure 10.10)
2. Run from home and round the corner at first. Practice the movements necessary to continue to second, or return to first.
3. Run from home to second base, creating a smooth angle around first base.

Figure 10.10

Figure 10.11

Leading Off

1. Stand on a base and take a lead. (Figure 10.11)
2. Practice returning to first base.
3. Practice breaking toward second base.
4. Practice reacting to the pitcher's pick-off move or delivery to the plate.

Baseball Talk: A Glossary of Terms

Like so many sports, baseball has a language all its own. Think a seed is something you plant in the garden? Think again! Over the next few pages, you'll be introduced to everything you need to know about the language of baseball. By the time you're done with this book, you'll not only be playing like a pro, you'll be talking like one, too!

Bang-bang play

A "bang-bang" play is a play that involves a close call, either on base or at home plate. The fielder is in position, the runner is running, the ball is in the air—which will arrive first?

Bender

A "bender" is pitcher-talk for a curve ball.

Bleeder

No, you haven't been transplanted to an emergency room. In baseball, a "bleeder" is a softly hit ball that somehow manages to avoid being caught.

Bloop

Baseball players have about a million ways to describe hits. A "bloop" is a weakly hit ball that forms an arc as it travels away from the plate.

Blue

Although this is a common nickname for umpires, try not to use it. You'll get better results if you call them by their name, or something more respectful, like "sir."

Check swing

A "check swing" usually happens when a batter changes his mind mid-swing. If the pitch isn't coming across the plate in the way he expected, the batter will hold back in order not to hit the ball.

Chopper

Yet another kind of hit, a "chopper" is a ball that bounces high off the ground. Choppers can be difficult for infielders to handle.

Chucker

Another name for the pitcher.

Double dip

You might hear commentators on television or radio talking about a "double dip." It's just baseball talk for a double-header—those rare occasions when one team plays two games in a row against another.

Excuse me swing

A close relative to the "check swing," an "excuse me swing" happens when a hitter takes a half-swing, or hesitates before swinging the bat.

Framing

Catchers will often "frame" a pitch when they're looking to trick the ump into calling a strike. The catch might be outside the strike zone, but the catcher will quickly move the ball over the plate and hope for the call! Sometimes it works, sometimes it doesn't.

Free pass

A hitter gets a 'free pass' to first base if he gets a walk.

Frozen rope

Here we go with the hits again: A "frozen rope" is a line drive that's hit hard. It travels quickly, and can be difficult to catch as a result.

Getting robbed

When a hitter talks about "getting robbed," he's usually complaining. He thought his hit was a sure thing—until the fielder made that terrific play.

Getting shaved

You might hear players on the bench say, "he shaved him" when the hitter taking his turn at bat has to duck or twist to get out of the way of a fastball thrown close to the face. Not a great feeling!

Hammer

Ballplayers have just as many names for pitches as they do for hits! A "hammer" is a sharply thrown curve ball.

Hill

Because it's built up to give the pitcher a better throwing angle, players often refer to the pitchers' mound as the "hill."

Hot box

A players in the "hot box" when he's caught in a run-down between two bases. A run-down usually ends up with the player being tagged out—unless the fielder makes a bad throw to his teammate!

In the hole

A ball hit "in the hole" will fly past the infielders to the right of the shortstop. This tends to be the most unprotected area of the field, and these hits will often drop in for a base hit.

Lid

Some people use the word "lid" to talk about a hairstyle; ball players use it to refer to their caps or helmets.

Mitt

This one's easy—a "mitt" is a baseball glove.

Pulled a string

More pitching terminology. When ball players talk about their pitchers' "pulling a string," they mean that a good change-up has been thrown.

Punch out

No, we're not talking about those rare bench-clearing brawls! A "punch out" is a called third strike. The term probably originated with the umpires' tendency to call the strike while making a punching motion with their arm.

Rocket

Like a frozen rope, a "rocket" simply refers to a hard-hit ball.

Rubber

The "rubber" is the plate found on the pitchers' mound. Look at page 18 if you want to know more.

Sanis

In the major leagues, players refer to their special sanitary socks at "sanis." Sanis can help ward off athlete's foot.

Scoop

A "scoop" is fielding play at first base. When a ball is thrown low by a fellow infielder, the first baseman has to scoop it out of the dirt.

Seed

A "seed" is a ball that's hit or thrown very fast. A pitcher who's "throwing seeds" is probably having a very good game.

Sink

A thrown ball has "sink" if it moves downward as it travels toward its target.

Slide piece

A "slide piece" is pitcher-talk for a slider.

Slugger

A "slugger" is a good power hitter—someone who routinely hits the ball over the fence. Mark McGwire is a sluggers; so is Sammy Sosa.

Southpaw

A "southpaw" is left-handed pitcher. There aren't that many of them in the major leagues, making them pretty valuable players.

Stopper

A "stopper" is a relief pitcher that comes in during the game's final inning to protect the lead. The New York Yankee's Mariano Rivera is one of the best stoppers in the major leagues.

Swipe

A player "swipes" a bag when he steals as base.

Tail

A thrown or hit ball is said to "tail" when it moves laterally as it travels. This can make it harder to catch.

Tater

This one's hard to figure out, but a "tater" is simply a home run.

Texas leaguer

Another strange one, a "Texas leaguer" is a ball that somehow manages to drop in for a hit—even though it shouldn't!

"The Show"

When minor league players talk about playing in the majors, they talk about going to "the show."

Tossed

If a player or a coach gets ejected from the game, he's been "tossed."

Turn two

A team that "turns two" has successfully completed a double play.

Tweener

A "tweener" is a ball that manages to squeak through the hole left between two infielders. Good for the hitter, frustrating for the fielders!

Wheels

Players talk about "wheels" when they are referring to another player's legs or speed. For example, "John's got great wheels." A player with wheels might do well in the outfield, or as a base stealer.

Baseball Resources

If you would like more information about recreational baseball in your area, contact one of the following organizations.

American Amateur Baseball Congress (AABC)
118–119 Redfield Plaza
Post Office Box 467
Marshall, Michigan 49068
Telephone: (269) 781-2002
Fax: (269) 781-2060
Email: AABC@voyager.net
Web: www.aabc.us
Progressive and continuous organized competition for preteens to adults, coordinated with other programs through USA Baseball and the American Baseball Coaches Association.

Babe Ruth Baseball
1770 Brunswick Pike
P.O. Box 5000
Trenton, New Jersey 08638
Telephone: (609) 695-1434
Fax: (609) 695-2505
Email: info@baberuthleague.org
Web: www.baberuthleague.org
Largest amateur baseball and softball program in the world with more than 800,000 players on 45,000 teams in 7,000-plus leagues around the world. Runs popular baseball camps.

Continental Amateur Baseball Association (CABA)
82 University Street
Westerville, Ohio 43081
Telephone: (740) 382-4620
Web: www.dbuck.homeip.net
Association of independent youth teams and leagues classified by age, with tournaments leading to state, regional, and world championships.

Dixie Baseball Inc.
P.O. Box 231536
Montgomery, Alabama 36123
Telephone: (334) 242-8395
Fax: (334) 242-0198
Web: www.dixie.org
Dixie Youth Baseball, Dixie Baseball Boys & Majors, and Dixie Softball.

Little League Baseball Inc.
P.O. Box 3485
Williamsport, Pennsylvania 17701
Telephone: (570) 326-1921
Fax: (570) 326-1074
Web: www.littleleague.org
League games, tournaments and camps worldwide.

National Amateur Baseball Federation
P.O. Box 705
Bowie, Maryland 20715
Telephone: (724) 262-5005
Fax: (724) 352-0214
Website: www.nabf.com
Email: NABF1914@aol.com
Established in 1914, this is the oldest continually operated national baseball organization in the U.S.A. Regional and national championship tournaments for 8 age divisions, from 10-and-under to unlimited.

USA Baseball
USA Baseball Headquarters
Hi Corbett Field
3400 East Camino Campestre
Tucson, Arizona 85716
Telephone: (520) 327-9700
Fax: (520) 327-9221
Web: www.usabaseball.com
Home of the U.S. Olympic, National, Junior National, Youth National and Junior Olympic teams.

Acknowledgments

I would like to thank several people without whom this book would not have been possible: Clare McKeon, who offered me this project and her support; Linda Pruessen, for guiding me in the right direction and helping to make my job so much easier—thanks for your patience, understanding and great organizational skills; photographer Chuck Kochman and his staff for their excellent work and endless patience; Craig Doherty, Sean Bignall, Kyle Young and Kelly Walker for their patience and great job during the photo shoot; Mike Bignall and Dave Doherty for coordinating kids and assisting with transportation to and from the photo shoot; Paul Godfrey, J.P. Ricciardi and the Toronto Blue Jays staff for supporting this project; the people from SkyDome for letting us use the field for the photo shoot.

Photo Credits

All photography in this book appears by permission of System 4 Productions, Inc., with the following exceptions: the photo on pages 10/11 appears by permission of Jed Jacobson/Getty Images, Inc.: the photos on pages 12 and 13 appear courtesy of the author; the photos on pages 16, 17, 24, 25, 26 and 27 appear by permission of the National Baseball Hall of Fame Library, Cooperstown, New York; the photos on pages 36 and 37 appear by permission of Baseball Canada; the photo on pages 38/39 appears by permission of Jeff Carlick/Getty Images, Inc.; the photos on pages 56/57 and 76/77 appear by permission of Al Bello/Getty Images, Inc.; and the photo on pages 94/95 appears by permission of Jonathan Daniel/Getty Images, Inc.

Index

drills, 82
warm-up exercises, 82
pitching rubber, *18,* 18
players
black, 17
cut-off, 72
positions, *20,* 21
minor league, 36
salary, 17, 36
substitutes, 21
playing catch, 28, 30–31, 45, 46 (*See also* throwing)
playing field, 18–19, *19*
popularity, baseball, 14
pop-ups. *See* fly balls
positive attitude, 98
practice, importance of, 13
practices, 33

Q
quadricep stretch, 41
quick hands (drill), 65

R
ready position (infielding), 58
ready position (outfielding), 69
receiving, 54–55 (*See also* catching)
drill, 92
registering to play, 32–33
relay drill, 75
relay person, 72
release points (throwing), 52–53
releasing ball, 50, 52–53
relief pitcher, 21
respect, 35
rest position (infielding), 58
rest position (outfielding), 69
right fielder, *20,* 21, 66
right-handed batters, 56
Rookie Ball, 33
rounders, 16
route running drill, 75
running on infield hit, 104
running on outfield hit, 105
runs, scoring, 20–21, 23

S
"sacrifice" situations, 99
safety, 30, 31 (*See also* equipment; injuries)
salary, 17, 36
sayings, 25, 27
Schilling, Curt, 78
scholarships, 37

scouts, 12, 37
seated toe reach, 41
second base, 18
second baseman, *20,* 21, 56
set position (pitching), 81
shadow swings (drill), 100
shin guards, 86
Shoeless Joe (Kinsella), 26
shortstop, *20,* 21, 56
shoulder stretch, 43
side end, 43
side to side hit, 63
signing up, 32–33
signs, catcher/pitcher, 76, 87
signs, coach/player, 106
sinking (fastball), 78
skull cap (catcher's), 86
SkyDome, 18
sliding in (baserunning), 107
slow rollers, 62
soft hit, 62
soft toss (drill), 101
songs, 26
Sosa, Sammy, 12
speed—player, 56, 62, 66, 76, 102, 106
speed—ball, 68, 78
sprints, 45
square stance (hitting), 97
"squeeze" play, 99
stadiums, 18
stance, hitting, 97
stationary catch, 50–51
"stay alive," 22
stealing bases, 23
stepping catch, 51
strategy, 24–25
stretching exercises, 40–45 (*See also* warm-up exercises)
strike, 22, 76
strike zone, 22, *22,* 76
substitute players, 21
swing (hitting), 98

T
tagging, 23, 61, 91
tailing (fastball), 78
"Take Me Out to the Ballgame," 26
T-ball, 33
Team Canada, 12
teammates, 33, 34
team stretches, 44–45
teams, 14
amateur, 17
benefits of playing on, 28

early history of, 16–17
signing up for, 32–33
teamwork, 25
television, 17
third base, 18
third baseman, *20,* 21, 56
three-finger cross-seam grip, 48
3/4 arm angle (releasing ball), 52–53
throat protector, 86
throwing, 30–31
from the outfield, 72–73
kneeling catch, 48–49
releasing ball, 52–53
stationary catch, 50–51
stepping catch, 51
throwing motion, 49
throwing progression drill (catchers), 93
throwing runner out, 60
timing
release of ball, 50
slide, 107
upsetting hitter's, 76, 79
top half, inning, 21
Toronto Blue Jays, 12
turn around (drill), 65
two-seam change-up, 79
two-seam fastball, 78

U
umpires, 21, 34, 35
under-arm release points, 52, 53
uniforms, 33
United States, 14, 16
universities, 37
upper 3/4 release, 52

V
visiting team, 21

W
"walk," 22
wall drill, 65
warm-up exercises, 38, 82 (*See also* stretching exercises)
weather, 21, 25, 35
whiffle ball (drill), 101
wind sprints, 45
World Championships, 12
World Series, 17

Y
Yankee Stadium, 18